9 to wine

Pihu's Diary

notionpress.com

9 to wine

Pihu's Diary

KHYATI SHARMA

Sketches by Sadhvi Sharma

notionpress.com

Notion Press

Old No. 38, New No. 6
McNichols Road, Chetpet
Chennai - 600 031
First Published by Notion Press 2016

ISBN 978-93-5206-644-5

Sketches by Sadhvi Sharma

Contents

Preface

Nine to Wine is the journey of a nine-year-old soul, Pihu, to her first wine glass. It talks of what a child learns in school, with her friends, while on vacations with parents, and while playing outside, on old streets. Pihu loves enunciating her life in the form of poetry and poetic prose. She reads them out to herself, whenever she feels like reliving all those years again.

Poetry in an age as young as nine may not be decorated with pearly words, but is seasoned with innocence. Innocence that sees beauty in everything: winters, fairies, tales of Cinderella. Innocence that is inculpable. She doesn't understand Sonnets or Limericks, but she loves to write for herself.

From there, begins Phase II of Pihu's life: her teens, where she starts experiencing different emotions. She experiences friendship, love, disappointment, envy and competition. The journey continues with disappointments of unattainable first love and falling hope. Pihu decides her way of life, and a way to success. She takes it as an answer to the challenges that life has thrown at her. She unlearns her fears and picks up the knack to focus on her growth. She becomes a star at school, then college and lands up in one of the best jobs.

Much to her surprise, she realizes that her soul doesn't agree to live a crude, unloving and pragmatic life. She tastes love again. She feels special and cared for. She makes him the centrifugal force of her life. She starts leading a life which wants him all the time - her soul mate. What she didn't know is that this was life's trap for her to fall. She fell, and this time, she fell hard, hard enough that she thought she lost her feet! She lost her self-belief. Her nine-year-old enthused soul gets shrouded with adult fears. From there begins a different revelation, one that shows how Pihu travels and unravels herself, and how she reboots her system and regains her enthusiasm.

The book shows the journey of her introspection and reflection through her diary and poems. It should be easy for readers to delve into the poems and take a step towards poetry and those thoughts that live on every day. Some of us are good at introspection. Some are good at expressing their thoughts. On the other hand, it is hard for some to articulate their experiences and lessons. I was inspired to write from everyday experiences, so that people can connect with the emotions they feel are real. We witness love, hope, disappointment, fear, courage, peace and many other emotions in our lives. We are not super-humans from movies with extraordinary powers and gadgets to survive adverse situations. We build our own tools to walk through life. The book brings to life all of those emotions through the story of a girl, Pihu, who makes her own way through life.

I hope you have a good time reading about Pihu's life through the poems and articles that she wrote from the time she was nine, right up to when she first tasted wine. The poems in the book are simple, yet deep. The language is subtle so that readers don't find it hard to read and understand the poems.

Acknowledgement

I owe the creation of this book to my mother. She always encouraged me to write and gave my diaries all the privacy they needed. She would read all the lines I wrote, even after long days, and sometimes, with weak eyes. Most of what I wrote was not even half as good as she would say it was, but her faith gave me the courage and strength to write with my heart and to write daily. All mothers trust their children's abilities, but what is special in my mother is that she was the only one who could see my water! What I mean by this is that she could see me as playful waves as well as high tides and deep oceans. She knew my faces and thoughts. She knew the future me right from when I was nine. I am still learning myself, but I guess she knows me fully.

Credit also goes to my *bade* papa (paternal uncle), who had faith in my writing. He carried the first set of ten poems I wrote in his briefcase all these years. By the way, the briefcase is a very special place in bade pa's life. It has spent the maximum time with him as he spent three-fourths of life traveling for business! Last but not the least, I would like to thank God for blessing me and giving me my sister. She always encourages me. But at the same time, she adds bounded rationality and sound criticism to my choices. She has lived through my dreams and fears. She has added a dimension of practicality to my choices. She has shielded me and guided me throughout my life.

Chapter One

Mumma's Sweetheart

Pihu was an inquisitive child. She always questioned whatever she didn't understand. All her summer vacations went in asking her mother the hows and whats of the world.

Her mother used to get her encyclopedias (back in the days when Google was not around) so that she could satiate her curiosity. She was always her mother's sweetheart! Her mother would often excuse her mischief saying, "She is just nine!" as an answer.

Pihu was a keen observer. She watched objects, people, and places with keen attention. She wouldn't miss a leaf skeleton on a roadside or the wrinkled face of an old man. She could visualize all lessons taught in school. If only she could draw, she would have created more episodes of the Jetsons! She grew up with the usual stories of the frog and the princess. But she wanted to speak out all that she saw. Her family was exhausted with her questions, and endless observations. Let us put it this way: listening to Pihu wasn't the usual marathon! It was a triathlon. Her teachers wrote "very talkative" year after year in her performance report.

She also liked to read. When she was eight, she became a fan of Enid Blyton. She used to read stories with pixies, red and blue mushrooms, and party tables with soufflés! She would get lost in Neverland. She wanted to be Peter Pan. She wanted to fly, play with colored marbles, and enjoy to the fullest extent. This was a phase when she was influenced by fairy tales. She used to read the thin booklets that her mother had got. All the time in the school bus, she would read the three little pigs, or the ugly duckling, or the snow queen. Stories of Goldilocks and Cinderella were bedtime tales. She would carefully see the pictures and let her mind imagine the rest.

Birthday Queen

The night before the big day quest,
Waiting for the pink, flowing dress
Dreaming of the chocolate mousse,
Party in the prettiest cruise,
Started dreaming, dreaming deep,
Pihu, the princess, in her dreamy sleep!
Riding a white horse, golden locks swaying
Below the hill top, elves' surprise is playing.
Micky and Minnie are making the cake,
Elves and pixies baking pudding and steak!
King and queen supervising the preps,
Excited Pihu dancing in quick steps
Broke her ankle woke up from sleep,
Finds her bedside with gift's heap!
Chocolates, gowns and her tiara,
Got ready for school like Princess Sara
Practiced to offer cookies to ma'am
'May I come in, my birthday' cram!
Her favorite Miss saw and called her in,
Kissed her birthday with a toffee tin.

Miss Tara

I go to school every day,
For you miss Tara I pray,
You like a white snowball,
You are pretty and tall,
Your smile is petals of a flower,
Your words shine like a star,
You don't shout and give us candy,
You smile when we forget Mandy.
I go to school every day,
For you miss Tara I pray,
When you go for holiday,
We plead hard with you to stay,
You gave me my first autograph.
You teach me beautiful craft.
I love to decorate boxes with you.
I love when you help me with glue.
For you I pluck roses from the garden.
I run fast in fear of the warden.
For you to school every day,
For you miss Tara I pray.

Fairies

I have read so much about fairies.
They give children chocolates from dairies.
Along with their magic sticks,
They perform different kinds of tricks.
Wearing a shiny white gown,
On woven magic carpets, they land down
Looking pretty, with a diamond crown,
To put smiles on sad faces, a fairy becomes a clown
Time for her to go back,
Homeless eyes waiting for magic on the track!

Pihu went on her first vacation. She went to the Shivaliks, a range in the Himalayas, with her parents, grandmother and her sister. They went in their favorite white car. Her father drove, and the drive lasted almost ten hours. The roads changed from the plains to the hills. The speed of the car and her father's vigilance on the road changed. Not just the roads, the temperature, trees, and even the kind of dogs changed. Pihu loved dogs! The street dogs on the hills were furry. She asked her father to stop the car, and picked up a puppy and caressed him.

In two days, she developed a routine in the resort. She would get up early to watch the sun rise. Every morning was cold and pretty. She loved the weather. It made her nose turn red. She thought she had a clown's nose! She did her first trek and was thrilled about it. The trek was narrow and muddy. Cold winds were whistling and shouting, as if they were calling out to her. She kept following the directions and walked faster. She could see snow-capped mountains. She walked fast, but realized how much easier it was to walk in the plains. She observed that all good and beautiful things don't come alone. Even nature had its way of telling her that a tremendous amount of hard work is required to see such beauty. But, she learnt this lesson much later in her life.

Winters

Morning rays touching the white,
The whites reflecting the yellow bright,
Walking fast in the smoke -
Wishing my finger could cloud poke!
Pines and cones sticking on my ballerina,
Shout to mountains and he calls me Pihu.
Gorgeous, the long river, half-frozen and half-clear
Men are trying with rafts to steer,
The chills freeze the hands and nose.
My mother gives soft wool clothes,
She knits them in white and pink.
I spill hot chocolate when I drink.
From the window, I am watching the sun set.
Orange on the snow, melting, slowly wet,
Nights are dark, foggy and lonely.
Everyone slept early, but the moon only…

Beauty of Nature

These lovely colorful flowers
They are deep, beauty drawers
These big green trees
Are feeding me and all the bees
This milky gorgeous moon,
Forcing me to finish the work soon
This is lush green grass
Compliments well with decors of brass
This yellow shining sun
Allows me to have fun
These sparkling stars in the sky
Are forcing me to say good bye
This beauty of nature I can't forget
This pity of God upon me is said

One day, Pihu was sitting in her school library. It was the library hour and she was busy reading a book by Enid Blyton, followed by a book from the Sweet Valley series. She started reading Sweet Valley ever since she saw the book in the hands of a gorgeous senior in the school bus. She thought of trying it out. Although she didn't like it much, she wondered if she should read another. Suddenly, the librarian appeared and asked Pihu if she wanted a book. The Miss was beastly. At times, she even appeared in Pihu's nightmares. She kept growing from the size of a pea to the size of a monster! Pihu was zapped. She saw the librarian holding a book by Jawahar Lal Nehru. She had instantly told her that it was the very book she was looking for! The librarian gave her a suspicious stare and issued the book on her card.

Pihu stared at the book with a sad face. She flipped through the pages. She was petrified! Suddenly, she told herself to try it, wondering how bad it could be. She started reading the book. To her surprise, she liked the genre! She read about incidents from the Revolt of 1857, right up to stories of Indian heroes who got India freedom. She came out of the world of fairies. She didn't want tiaras any longer. She wanted to fight battles! She wanted to find the purpose of her life. She experienced her first patriotic feelings.

Rani Lakshmi Bai

Maharani Lakshmi Bai, A great woman
Who defeated all the British men,
She played not with dolls, but bows and arrows,
She worked on resolving her people's sorrows.
Riding on the horse was her hobby
Instead of cleaning the lobby
She was married to the King of Jhansi
But the British treated her as a *dasi*
After her son's death
The legacy of the empire became a short-lived breath
She fought with the Brits bravely
She did her best to not surrender to slavery
She was one of the best freedom fighters we had
Her sacrifice was inspiring not sad!

India in My Dreams

India in my dreams is full of wonder,
Watching its greatness, the skies thunder!
India – full of purity and simplicity,
India – full of equality and secularism,
Is India of my dreams.
India in my dreams is full of wonder.
Watching its greatness, the skies thunder.
India – full of technology,
India – full of development,
Is India of my dreams.
India in my dreams is full of wonder,
Watching its greatness, the skies thunder,
India – free from corruption,
India – free from social evils,
India – free from pollution,
Is India of my dreams.
India in my dreams is full of wonder,
Watching its greatness, the skies thunder.

I Hate Math

It's Monday again - 12:00-13:00.
Math Miss on her way, I dread,
She will teach us each integer,
The battle of fraction/integer – is her teaser.
Integer increases when squared,
Fraction when squared is barred.
I don't follow a sum at her speed,
She cleans the board faster than I breathe.
12:00-13:00 – it's Tuesday.
Homework not done, punishment in tray,
Standing outside the class, I peep inside.
Today's topic - LCM on slide.
Q. LCM of 4 and 12 write,
I calculate with my pencil on wall white,
Wanted to answer first to get away from plight,
I yell, 4*12 = 48 with my hand uptight,
I run towards my seat thinking the answer is right.
When miss tells me it's not 48 but 12.
She tells me to study harder and there rings the bell,
Lunch time it is, I don't care about Math,
Next period is history, I will score a pat.

Teens
Chapter 2

Teen Trouble

Pihu has moved ahead in life - a little away from her mother's lap, but closer to her friends' claps. She is in her teens now.

The beauty of nature, the innocence of holidays, and the love for teachers are all substituted with a few friends. She calls them friends, but neither they nor she care too much for each other. They stick together for the need to associate, the need to belong. We all have seen those days in our life.

She likes someone deeply, though. His name is Rahul. He thinks beyond the school, and an empty, vanity ridden life. He is smart, intelligent, and deep. He reminds her of her hidden self. He loves to write as much as she does. She spends a lot of time, admiring him secretly. He was the reason she went to school. She found excuses to stay close to him. She picked up similar hobbies. Table tennis tournaments were her favorite event. The reason was that he was in the school team. He could serve in fourteen ways. She could barely manage one. She practiced hard to impress him every day.

She elected for physics and maths, a subject she hated, to keep him in her line of sight. They became good friends. They started practicing for hours for the tournaments.

She loved listening to hm articulate his thoughts, ideas and philosophies. When he tried to explain why Pascal's triangle was the best ever discovered theory, or how one can serve in fourteen ways while playing table tennis, or what friends are for, everything seemed like the guiding channel of life for her. She believed his theories. She looked at life from his perspective, most of the time. Such was his influence. That was exactly how love had to be defined or expressed. It was also a function of his explanation.

Love

One can feel this,
One can express this,
I hope love may be this.
When one comes nearer,
And becomes dearer,
I hope love may be this.
One can multiply this,
One can divide this,
I hope love may be this.
Sharing joys and sorrows,
And the sorrows we borrow,
I hope love may be this.
When ones heart shines,
And he thinks it is very fine,
I hope love may be this.
Dreaming about this,
Thinking all about this,
Wandering all around,
Now I have found,
Love can only be this.

It's This

Saying no and no to this,
But I had to bow to this,
Something so fine like this,
Something so kind like this.
No quarrels in this,
Only affections, its bliss,
No castes or tribes in this,
No age or bribes in this,
No hits and no beats,
Hope all are out to seek,
Climbing the mountain peak.
Moving in scorching desert creeks,
I did finally FIND 'This'.

But, she was far away from letting him know those thoughts. She was possessed and shielded by love, her first love! She started reading Keats and listening to Frank Sinatra.

However, she knew it was hard for her to spread her arms and get it.

She was close to being disenchanted. She was deep in the waters, and yet, she was floating. She knew, soon, she would be close to sinking! Her prayers had him more than her own happiness. But all philosophies on experiencing love and not having it offered her no condolence. She wanted it and badly at that. After all, she slept and woke up with these thoughts for almost four years now! While mornings began with prayers, nights ended with sad and lonely, romantic songs, on loop. Her pillow was wet with the void.

She struggled with dilemma between whether she had to tell Rahul or just live the friendship she had. She knew that he had many admirers and fans at school. She didn't want to be on that pedestal. She wanted more! He was not just someone she wanted, but also someone she looked up to. But everything was shattered when she discovered the two sides – the Dr. Jekyll and Mr. Hyde – that lived in Rahul. He lived a dubious life. He was deep, yet shallow. He easily gauged the likes and dislikes of girls around him and offered conversations, gifts, help or whatever made it possible for him to stay close. When she confronted him with this truth, all he said was, "Pihu! Fans are important for head-boy elections! I can't help if people like me. You've been the nicest fan. If you stay loyal to me, I can get you any guy you want!"

Everything paused for almost a year. She expresses her love, her rage and her disappointment in her poems and music. Both of these offered her calmness.

When You Left Me

Pain in the heart,
Grief in the heart,
There is a big void,
Like no Madonna, no Floyd,
Bees, no buzz,
Flowers, no smile,
Paintings, no color,
Songs, no music,
Existence, not life,
Steep trek, no balance,
Water, no oxygen,
Food, no hunger,
Who Madonna, Who Floyd,
All void,
Pain in the heart,
Grief in the heart.

What Happens When You Don't Get It

Wanted to feel the touch on untouched,
Wanted to ruffle the un-ruffled hair,
Wanted to taste the depth of the inedible,
What do you get, When you don't get it!
You get something - something else,
To feel the pain, the helplessness,
To feel the attractive repulsion,
To feel the pull to stay close and away
You get more… Something more.
To dance on the staged stage,
To pray to the 'director' for a roll change,
To bribe 'Him' for promises,
You are left with an empty hand,
Neck and hands stringed and *puppetted*
Searching for invaluables to fill the pot
Willing to burrow in the alms.

My Value

My value is null for you,
Like with rose a thorn grew,
Mere member of your fan club,
Our conversations seem a snub.
Don't want to bait other girls,
Don't want to twist in your curls,
Wanted more meaning and depth,
Got left with confidence, leaning,
I feel weak with you,
Dead, drained, and blew!
I feel used as a shoulder,
Your feelings grew colder,
You didn't stay a warm friend,
You got close to set a trend,
Like with rose a thorn grew,
My value is null for you!

The Self-Respect Glass

The morning mirror shone with self love
It reflected the smile of 'the' feeling.
The light of him illuminated my face,
The love whispers added to the blush.
Suddenly, it has become hazy -
I am trying to find the smile.
Wiping the haze with your sympathy,
No love, but am ready even for pity!
The sun rose and set, but no light reflects,
Mirror stays hazy, with no shine!
One ray, somehow, cracked till the mirror
And I saw…
The broken self-respect glass.

The Vindictive Accusations

Despair and disappointment turn,
'Vindictive' feelings now burn.
Dilated pupils have formed a roar,
With blame words are sore.
You're the reason for my first pain!
You're the cause of self disdain!
All efforts and patience went in vain,
Try to fix but cracks remain!
You could read it in my eyes,
Yet you chose to leave over cries!
Dark or bright your color is addictive,
Love stronger and reshaped to vindictive

Life is a Ride on a Horse

Can't be learnt from a book
Can't contain the horse with a look
Takes hard to reach a saddle,
Need to make your way to the riddle.
Takes skill, tolerance, and balance,
Horse and rider need to have valence.
An ounce here and there you feel fall,
Each fall teaches what to do,
A hundred try, not all catch the clue.
Every long ride leaves pain in the back,
But need to ride to see what you lack,
Important lesson is to trust your horse.
If he feels the valence, it eases the force,
He is stronger, still lets you control,
Wants you to feel the pulse and soul,
Once you unite, it's an adventure,
Hidden beautiful trails you venture,
Enjoy the pain control the ride,
Determination helps cross a tide.

Chapter 3

Aisha - Her Anchor

Pihu's sister. Aisha was her anchor. She saw her torment every day. She knew that Pihu was talented, but was not doing her best. She was curious to understand why, and wanted to help her. She didn't know how, though. Pihu was not willing to share much. Out of helplessness, one day, Aisha decided to read Pihu's diary.

She spent the whole night, screening through the pages, while Pihu was asleep. But to her surprise, Pihu had anticipated such behavior. She had written everything in code. She developed her own script, where all alphabets were boxed - enclosed in lines drawn on all sides - in a way that every letter looked like a box. Aisha decoded her sister's language trick. She read and re-read the whole diary all night, and finished it around 7:00 AM.

Pihu woke up for school and couldn't find her diary. She knew what had happened as soon as she looked at Aisha's damp eyes, filled with love and concern. Pihu broke down. She hugged Aisha tight. She didn't have to say a word. Aisha knew she was begging for help. Both took an off from school and talked at length.

Aisha wanted to be of help and yet, not sound like a rigid parent. She figured that Pihu needed a boost. She needed to focus on a different path, but with the same goals. She told Pihu to focus on self-improvement with a guarantee, that she could get all she wanted after all the hard work.

She explained that a year of hard work would change Pihu and help her achieve her needs. Pihu didn't completely understand Aisha, but went on to introspect and work harder. She enjoyed the entire journey and thrill to see the changed person that she was. Her teen years actually became hopeful and sanguine.

Question Letter

Reach your heart
And your words start.
Start with questions
And answer each with emotions.
Just go on…
Who are you?
For whom all do you do?
Who cares for you?
What is your wish?
Are you a water-scant fish?
Do you know what to do next?
Is your value like a worthless pest?
Who needs you and why?
Many other questions just go on.
Answer your questions till the next dawn,
Next night, again, put your heart in a question letter.

What I Want Now

Not me, at least, for this job
I just want to stop.
I want to improve myself,
God, help me reach this high shelf!
I want to move away from negative things,
Keep me away from such beings
Help me concentrate on my work
Help me work hard without a jerk.
Why am I bored of studying?
Why can't my brain do math-loading?
Why you don't help me?
Show me the right path if I am not able to see!
I want to achieve my goal,
I want to be a proud soul,
I want success in my life first,
For this my social life I can burst.
Up in the sky, I want to show it to my father,
Where he praises me and not blame me rather.
High above on moon I want to land,
God, all disturbances from my life be banned.

Confidence Recipes

Don't you worry,
For failure is not the judge.
Experience would add,
For not trying would grudge.
Forget the outcome,
For it adds to fear.
You can be confident,
For it just takes to dare.
Trying more adds to rise,
For others don't get to know.
Experience makes you a star,
For aspirants to bow.
Try to know and think more,
For knowledge doesn't waste.
Observe life and people carefully,
Don't run a half hearted race.

Motivated, Pihu started thinking deeply for herself. She was charged with positivity. Every day, after school, she would stay back and practice for her debates. She realized that she never really enjoyed table tennis. She had just taken it up for Rahul.

She had more to herself than Rahul! The harder she practiced, the better she was getting, at her oratory skills. She put her mind and heart in her studies. She won almost every competition that she took part in. She traveled around Delhi, Bombay, Jalandhar and Noida to attend various forums. She became a star.

People knew her across school and in the education fraternity. She remembered her inspirational models, namely, Rani Jhansi, Aisha, and her mother, whenever she thought she would give up. That would give her strength to go on longer.

Other kids at school started seeking advice from her. Most underdogs wanted to know ways for transformation. She was not as articulate, then, to explain everything. But she told them to have faith in their capability and to first work for themselves.

She also told them to stay positive and trust God, and the form he sent - as one's parents and family. She couldn't forget the days when she thought her mother was not the same generation as her and wouldn't understand the pain of these feelings.

She used to feel that Indian society had evolved in the past 30 years. Everyone's talk on the generation gap misguided her on her mother's instincts and care. But the valleys of life made it clear that mothers stay strong for their children. It was not as clear to her, but she had a sense of guilt with regard to her slight rebellious behavior.

She had seen how her mother stood for her, for every single competition. Her mother took her from one city to another.

She lost her pay, took leave, ate less, and wore the same set of clothes, all so that Pihu could compete without an issue.

Pihu's faith in herself and God was restored. She understood that one critical aspect of the generation gap was that children oddly get rebellious and parents still stand by them. Her senior years at school were filled with moments of respect for her mother and with values of hard work, patience and humility.

Divine

I have been very grateful to you,
Oh God! I came late to you,
But I came to you.
Keep my promise – which I would do,
You did what you did, for betterment of mine,
You kept things away, for my character to shine.
I am in trouble, what is DIVINE?
It is devotion and a feeling to be felt,
But not something to be defined in a line.
You picked my hand - small,
You handed me my lost red ball,
You walked me in all
To the dreary desert, in the marshy lands,
You saved me from lizards and sands,
You showed the right path first,
You relieved me from my thirst,
When due to sun, my skin burnt.
Then weather from hot to pleasant turned,
You always have a hand on my head.
You invited sweet dreams when I was in bed,
By this I can tell myself, you will never forget,
For this with anyone I can have a bet.

Mother's Care

When I needed you,
You were never there.
When I was scared,
You were never there.
When I required a love layer,
You were never there.
But when I turned behind,
You were so fine.
That for me in pain you were crying,
The sun that fell on me, first fell on you.
The water that sunk me, first carried you,
I couldn't recognize your care.
My heart feels all the care we share.

Want To Grow Fast

Mother, you work night and day,
You slip to work before the first ray.
I see the cracked heels,
I see the soft and steel,
I see the early worry wrinkles,
I see the fading forehead and lost twinkle,
I see the counting of pennies for school,
I see you dealing alone with the world cruel,
I see the easy life you could have had,
I see the role you play: mom and dad.
I wish I grow faster to be your stick,
I wish I soon bandage every prick,
I would work hard to succeed,
I apologize for all the pain and bleed.
Mother you work night and day,
I could fulfill your dreams I pray.

51
2
1
3

Today I Have

Today, I have
A wave of
Happiness,
Of bliss.
Today I have
A wish,
To fly,
In the sky.
Today I have
A will,
To be the best,
To reach the crest.
Today I have,
A dream,
To twinkle
When I wrinkle.
Today I have
A hope
To have
A dream
A will
A wish
A wave,
Every tomorrow.

Pihu's upbeat energy and positive attitude made her the head prefect at school. She was the best. An all-round girl, she was always involved in diverse activities.

It was that time of the year when results were to be released, and uncertainty was at peak. Pihu had done well. She was in the top five, at school. She took her entrance exams and got into one of the finest colleges in Delhi University.

She had chosen commerce over engineering. She was good with business administration and business ideas. The environment at her college was different from that at school. The college was successful at screening the competitive minds. People wanted to make it big in life. There were some who read The Economic Times while sipping on cola. There were some who fought over business politics, but some, who whiled away in canteen.

Pihu was determined as ever. She decided to continue doing all of it. She read The Economic Times, studied as well as whiled away time at the local canteen and the milkshake shop, which served hot dumplings and noodles with milkshakes. It was a perfect spot to hang out in the evenings, for students in the college.

Life was slightly different. She was far away from home, and traveled by the metro, carried her own phone, and got travel and food allowance.

This was her first encounter with saving money. She was not interested in clothes, shoes, and make-up like other girls were. She wanted to pay for music lessons, watch movies, attend fairs and see new places.

UNIVERSITY

Undergrad Accident

DU and its marvel
Crowd worth the travel,
Girls dressed swanky
From Stephens to Venky,
My college out of escapade -
Professional and disciplined it stayed.
No ragging, little bragging
Discipline and academic nagging,
Thought of Hindi movie institute,
Landed in black and white, mute,
Every three months, books turned around,
Every student intellectually sound,
Yet, it taught many lessons,
It brought grey to fashion,
How to live simple and high,
How to run without sigh,
It taught the freedom,
Tagore wrote and did strum
Mind without fear, Head held high
Bleed business for things money can buy

Living Chindi

Days when pockets are empty,
But true friends are senti.
When one lunch box feeds plenty,
When you spy friends' food inventory.
Each chindi college day,
In everyone's heart they stay,
Days when Rs 50 meant recharge,
When in buddies' room you simply barge,
When pants didn't need crease and starch,
When a Maruti could fit 15 large,
Each chindi college day
In everyone's heart they stay.
Days when your juniors didn't look you in eye,
When you needn't look for shoulders to cry
When you borrow Rs 40 for burger and fry,
When you drank hoarded *daru* on days dry,
Each chindi college day
In everyone's heart they stay.
Days when friends partner in crime,
When they call you at any time,
When they pick you sloshed and feed lime,
When you divide the mass bunk fine,
Each chindi college day
In everyone's heart they stay.

Placement Fever

Middle class dreams and Money,
Placement season can be sunny.
A month before the drama begins,
We wake before the sleep ends.
Cram all numbers to estimate cases,
Become mannequins, tie our laces.
Business, economics and Government policy,
Beat the bush on logical fallacy.
Dreams of big cabins and suits,
High salary and other fruits.
Parents' dreams and pressure,
Money society's funnel and measure.
Sharmaji's daughter and six-digit cheque,
Didn't matter her health in wreck.
Kohli's son gets a joining car.
Our children would be bigger star.
So some secretly join prep class,
While some relax with grass.
Everyone rolls their sleeves,
Idealizing the Buffets and Steves.
One percent gets placed by day zero,
Others envy the mass hero.
Blame companies and question hires,
Placecomm gets subjected to satires.

By day ten, everyone has a job,
Suddenly all alike, no one is a snob.
Middle class dreams and money,
Placement season ends with honey.

Wine

A fresh leaf out of Pihu's book is always like breathing in the morning sun. She started working and learning the new ways of a corporate life. She was at her first job, far away from home. She was willing to explore diversity. She wanted to meet new people, work hard, party harder, and manage on her own. She was away from Aisha and her angel mother. But she was in love with this change.

Getting up in the morning and running to work with breakfast in hand, a day full of coffee and merger models, a night full of salus and cheers! She took her first step to the next phase of her life: wine.

Chapter 4

I am a Lady

Life was smooth. She was living her dream job. Her school and college teachers were proud of her job and achievements. She had become independent monetarily. She was twenty-five. She could see the change in herself. She had stopped drinking straight from beer bottles many years ago. Her tangled hair had become beautiful, and her locks had grown long. There was no space for any bobbed hair in her lady friends' circle. Her wardrobe had changed from grey and black Linkin' Park t-shirts to whites and peaches. She moved from Nike to Juicy Couture and Manolo Blahniks.

She understood the meaning of pumps and a Louis Vuitton bag. She understood why her mother insisted on smiling pleasingly and gently. She was turning into a fine young lady.

Blood and Sweat

First job is like barren land,
Needs work from ground zero to stand.
Ambition to succeed in boiling blood,
Sow seeds of hard work in irrigated mud.
Forgetting pain and Sleep, early rise,
Gamble personal life on roll of dice.
Work hard from twelve to sixteen hours,
Can only feel LED no sun no stars.
Obstacles of rain and rework,
Perseverance to start again and not duck.
Not get bowled over by bullies and bosses,
Starve, cut expenses, survive losses.
Out in the world of pests and eagles,
Stands the scarecrow strong and fickle.
All the hard work and there comes the first sprout,
First pay cheque answers all about.

No More Beer

My toes painted and filed,
My hair long and styled,
I dress in white and peaches,
No more beer at beaches.
Bermuda and baggies gone,
Football jerseys away drawn,
Interest and hobbies changed,
Nine foot long wardrobe ranged
Wine parties with girls,
Sports bar no more ma world,
Exhilarated about dates,
Life laying a sweet bait.
Blush at compliments,
Tears at sentiments,
Pearls my favorite stars,
Lilies my favorite flowers.
Learnt to smile soft,
Shoe heels like a loft,
Saturdays are for high tea,
Turning to a lady, maybe.

Grown Up Me

I work hard and handle money,
Mom no more the finance attorney.
Toning my speech and eye contact,
I am prepared to take corporate wreck.
Sipping coffees to get breakthroughs,
Pulling my team strong through the brews.
Weeks get longer but I don't care,
Cost for growth I m ready to bear.
I talk less and speak more,
I observe every knock and door.
I chose to work than knock,
Got self-belief harder than rock.
I manage to fit in yet stay me,
I know Manolos yet fit the floaters.
My work speaks for me,
I don't need an LV!

Corporate Shenanigan

Work hard to get a reward,
Work smart to get it fast.
If you have it, you'll make It blast,
Initial days charm you into it.
Taste of fresh Lavazza,
Parties with nachos and masa,
Big cabins and cubicles,
Shackle you tight.
Pseudo-comfort seems right,
Bugs start creeping in soon,
Licking is heavier than creating,
Improper updates on rating,
It's a maze find the path,
Hack the system and make life easy,
Create, lick and become sleazy,
Long before you'll know.
You're a corporate slave,
BMW and firangi trips you crave,
Others seem dumb if you hack,
You grew on multiplying backs,
You definitely up skill this knack,
Feel like a king if you're this kind,
Stink of stagnation, find other find,
King or slave, it's your skill and mind.

Jacketed and suited bodies walked about with plastic smiles. Some had far better technical skills than she did. Some worked their way through networking. They had the talent of passing off their fake smiles as the world's most caring ones. Stories of people offering favors to their bosses were not uncommon. There were many kinds of favors: some would shop for their bosses' kids or offer their contacts or would buy gifts while on international tours and such else. The world worked like that, could she complain? She had many questions in her mind. Did networking outweigh other skills? What should she work on next – her technical skills or her networking skills? Should she ensure transparency or leverage the information asymmetry?

Her biggest struggle was to understand gender stereotypes. Why were more men getting hired? How was a man marrying different from a woman marrying? Why was it that a man working five hours a day and whiling away the other five hours smoking cigarettes, was deemed better than a married woman who worked efficiently for eight hours, and sought to head home to care for her children after that? She knew that some women were not great performers but that was also the case among men. She could see that men were impatient about their growth that they often comprised the attrition basket!

Shouldn't women be considered to be more committed? Probably women needed to be more upfront about their work commitments and marketing skills. They needed to stop trusting fairness of rewards and bosses and fight their way up the ladder more ruthlessly. Even better, they should hone their drinking and smoking skills, for that would reward them with a better bonus. She didn't have answers. She knew that all questions could not be answered in a go.

She decided to make peace with the turbulence. Pihu tried to do the best she could. She set herself as the benchmark. She stopped comparing her efforts and rewards with those of others. She decided to focus on delivering and not getting involved in politics. She looked at other people only as examples or warnings. She took reality with a pinch of salt. She lost interview battles to those who were less skilled, but offered favors. She suffered a couple of times, since she was not in the so-called "in" group. She introspected for a reality check. She knew she didn't want to offer favors. This meant that her growth would be stunted. Unless, she completely overdid her work hours or brought complete novelty to the table. She decided to make it her responsibility to get over the gender bias at work in her career in the long-term.

Pihu started working with introspection. She brought a special sauce to her work. She faltered with obvious solutions, but she was great at creative problem solving. Her godfather at work knew this. He knew he wanted a diverse team with different skill sets. She learned that "diverse" was the most overrated word in the corporate world. But it did offer benefits when one brought something special to table. It could be their commitment, ideation, technical skills and such else. Most "intelligent" managers did recognize the reality that they couldn't run a team with just good networkers. They needed hard working and skilled people.

Pihu could develop new products and solutions. However, her greater and deeper grasp of the system only brought disappointment. She grew because of her skill, though she could see many who were not-so-skilled, growing faster than her. Some were in the "in" group, so it was understandable. But some could scare the managers with their tempers. They were the difficult to handle, pseudo-star-performers. This was a surprising group! She didn't see the fairness. She figured out the corporate shenanigans.

She started progressing on work-life balance. It usually happens when one realizes that the corporate hullaballoo is not worth all those hours without progress in their personal life. She decided to put in just the required effort, in line with the Pareto

Principle. Everyone says that 20% of the things influence 80% of the result. She prepared to socialize in balanced time. She wanted to explore all the new cafes in Gurgaon and catch up with her old friends. She stirred her corporate life up with her hard and smart work. She was gaining above average growth with this strategy.

Chapter 5

It happens again

Time was running fast and so was Pihu's first car. She was with him, listening to a track which connected them instantly.She was not aware of what life had planned for her. Right now, she just cared about the Pakistani singer, the rolled-down windows and shaking her head to the music. The ease and fun was obvious. They were together in college. The drives multiplied and so did their interest in each other. She knew him for five years but never thought she would ever think of him in any way different from that of a friend. The question of *"Is it happening again?"* brought her back to the writing table.

The highways started to seem like bliss. She got to spend more time with Neel. They took turns to drive to work. They were bonding well. It was the perfect time to be in love, in Delhi andin the winter. There was mist and fog, it was straight out of a Bollywood movie! Songs, mist, the speed of the car, the warmth of the kulladh (earthen cup) tea and long conversations.

The conversations extended to movies every Friday, most often, first shows, trying new food centers from the roadside noodle truck to posh Italian dinners in South Delhi and Connaught Place from Tonnino to Magique and Cibo.

Pihu liked Neel's ambitions, his style of speaking, his chivalryand his eyes. His eyes pierced hers. All she could manage was to shy away from his gaze. But was this love or just attraction? Was he the right guy? Were they spending enough time together? Could he just see the fun-loving side of her, or could he look deeper into her at the innocent Pihu, who refrained from falling in love?

She didn't know…

Sweet Pain

It's strange but true,
I am in love with you.
Every moment I wait to talk,
Close my eyes and remember your walk.
Though it has not been long,
Yet the feeling is so strong.
It's strange but true,
I am in love with you.
Recall our casual talk a million times,
But every word in it sings love rhymes.
Every word you say seems so right,
A little smile from you and my world ignites.
It's strange but true,
I am in love with you.
I don't know if you feel the same,
It's scary alone to take the blame.
Touch of togetherness is worth the pain,
I am ready to ready to flow and drain.
It's strange but true,
I am in love with you.

The Journey

It began with an exchange of looks.
Constant peeping through souls, that's all it took.
You and I knew it inside,
Our hearts tickled at every sight.
Was waiting for your words, not just looks,
But all pages you wrote made empty books.
I explained myself to be patient and give time,
You were not expressive enough for the climb.
I wanted to talk and clear your issues,
I wanted to better understand your clues,
I could see love in your eyes but it wasn't spoken,
I knew you had some reservation,
The journey reached its cross road.
You had the option to leave or speak and board,
I know the latter required courage,
We knew our weaknesses: our love and rage,
Friends that we were, added to the confusion stir,
Turbulence at halt, you decided to be what you were,
My hurt gave you the courage to move.
A journey where you don't need to prove,
We would discover everything on the way,
We would walk together in dark and in ray,
Eyes meet and souls align,
The journey continues and it is divine.

Soulmate

No one has ever done what you have done for me,
I love the way, my soul, you can see.
In love, it is not just important to be together,
But feel each other's presence rather.
I never believed this until I met you,
Love is not about being "Me" but one in "two."
No one has ever done what you have done for me,
I love the way my soul you can see.
There is a lot of baggage we all carry in life,
It gets difficult to continue with it in further strive.
But you try to take some from me on your shoulders,
You try to suppress from my way all boulders.
No one has ever done what you have done for me,
I love the way my soul you can see.
At times, life gets stressed,
My soul mate, your presence gets pressed,
I might question the depth of love then.
But I remember your presence, you were around when,
Then, my heart repeats to my mind:
No one has ever done what you have done for me,
I love the way my soul you can see.

Pihu was on cloud nine. Her ambitions had kept her away from the taste of such a relationship all her years in college and high school. She made Neel her mission and goal. Fanatically, she chalked out their plans in the form of a time table.They would meet at 8:00 AM, then at 12:00 PM, and then 7:00 PM. Neel was equally enthused. He didn't want to let her go out of his sight. They efficiently finished office work and left on time. Weekends were planned with more depth and were detailed. There were exchange of Excelsheets with options and preferences. Every date was meticulously thought of. There were movies, dinners, operas, plays and parties. These were not cricket matches or Gurgaon theatres that Pihu would go to, dressed in T-shirts and shorts. These were posh gala events, which often involved Neel's colleagues and the snobbish crowd.

Neel was very socially conscious. He always dressed up appropriately with his hair combed to perfection. Pihu had to shape herself to reflect Neel. She was somehow convinced directly or indirectly by Neel that there was nothing wrong with more grooming. She agreed. She worked on her wardrobe, her hairstyle, and at times, even her accent. While their plans to go a wine tasting were shaping up, their meetings were interrupted by a small pause.

Neel had his first project outside India for six months. Pihu was very supportive. She wanted Neel to grow. Neel respected Pihu for this. They decided to chat on Skype everyday and exchange emails. All was going well. Pihu was writing her bit of emails regularly. But Neel was finding it hard to cope. There was the pressure of a new country and a new role. People and expectations were different. Moreover, the weekends were reserved for travel to the country side as well as to European cities. The pressure, exposure and excitement was creating a new Neel.

The good news in grey was that his bosses were about to offer him permanent stay in the European head office. However, she wasn't quite sure of the degree of 'good.' Pihu wanted to discuss Neel with her family once he got back. Neel had agreed. But now, it seemed that Pihu may have to relocate. She started exploring her professional options.

When Neel got back, she went to pick him up at the airport. On the way back, he bragged about Europe and life abroad. He didn't sound like himself. He was not as keen on the kind of work he would get there but the fact that he could buy a second BMW and how cool it would look. Pihu didn't mention to Neel, that she despised Indians who thought working outside India was better than in India. She was about to share her work options in Europe, but suddenly, something inside her stopped her. She went ahead and asked Neel if he would be willing to stay in India for her, especially if she got a better opportunity in India, better than what Neel and Pihu had as of now. He looked at her and refused outright. He wanted to go.

For the first time, Pihu felt that she didn't have the courage to pursue the discussion further. With the urge to appeal Neel, she told him about her research and options in Europe and they both discussed it happily.

She knew that she had dropped the ball somewhere. She, the binder of her friends, talked little with them now. She featured less in all fun pyjama parties everyone had together. Work and one relationship were enough for her to handle. Pihu caught up less with her family too. She centered her life on these very absorbing aspects of her relationship with Neel. She didn't realize this until this relationship failed. Neel's trip to Europe and appetite for more of it had outgrown his future with Pihu. Even after arriving at sound and agreeable plans, Neel was demonstrating repulsion.

She got lonelier by the day. She started finding faultwith herself. She was told she had those extra pounds that she couldn't shed. She was told her hair couldn't make a bun as beautiful as he wanted. She was told she didn't wear red enough number of times. She tried to shop for more red. But it wasn't her color! She tried to starve but her work didn't let her lose those pounds. Neel had no patience and decided to quit this before Pihu could take one more step in any direction. He left for Europe without telling her. One of his friends was kind enough to tell her one day to tell her that he had gone, not to come back. His third sentence was – "You should move on."

Pihu had invested so much in this relationship. She wanted it back. She constantly tried Neel's numbers. She left messages on Facebook. Her emails implored him to be back. She was addicted to his presence and her dreams with him. She had changed so much for him that she didn't understand herself anymore. She would stand in front of the mirror and remain unrecognized.

She didn't know how to get back, now. She had lost her way. She had lost her enthusiasm.She had forgotten how to make friends. She was so comfortable with her one-dimensional life that she didn't know how to deal with the change. She wanted herself back, but didn't know how. Aisha was not around. She was busy with her really challenging goals and dreams. Pihu didn't want to disturb her. She thought this time, it was just her and her wine. She spent months thinking and staying away from the world.

She knew she had grown up and the world expected her to behave in a certain way. She chose work as a hideout. She started putting in nights. Her days at work were as long as twenty hours a day. She got noticed at her workplace. But she knew she was empty. All the progress was, of course, tangible, but she was empty within.

Respect Over Love

Lost myself in love,
Did I?
Changed to suit your arms,
Did I?
Redefined my purpose as you,
Did I?
Weighed my love in gold,
Did you?
Sold the soul for a sexy hound,
Did you?
Traded plain eyes for loud mascara,
Did you?
Auctioned my pain for pounds,
Did you?
Call again and beg to get back,
Shall I?
Get drunk to resist the lack,
Shall I?
Recite the mighty togetherness,
Shall I?
Chose love over respect,
Shall I?

Life Is A Deep Red Scar

The cheeks which stayed pink,
Turned pale and blue.
The talks that never ended,
Could not find their clue.
The smile which was contagious,
Lost its length and glue.
The hopping and jumping feet,
Could not find their stand.
The healing and nurturing touch,
Could not feel its hand.
The soulful clear deep eyes,
Got dusted with doubtful sand.
The rising graph went circular,
And the solid center moved far.
The innocent honest promises,
Couldn't match the pragmatism bar.
The ever optimistic hopeful white,
This time got a deep red scar.

Lost

Lost that I am, can't find myself back,
Can't find the power for pessimistic shackles to crack,
Can't find the spirit and enthusiasm,
Can't dig myself buried in sarcasm,
Can't find the rolling stone that I was,
Moss is all I see, the stone did pause.
Why did the stone pause?
Why does the clock tick, and can't cross?
Why can't the running feet walk?
Why has the bird lost its flock?
When would, myself, I find?
When would I come out of grind?
When would hope crop?
When would the rain drop?
Lost that I am, can't find myself back,
Can't find the power for pessimistic shackles to crack.

Chapter 6

The Great Depression 2013 and its end

The prose details her journey from the poem "Lost" to "The ET Way" (which comes in the next chapter)

The Great Depression (Phase I):

She was lost in life for a couple of years, now. Life seemed to betray her at various points: failure of certain planned professional goals, her inability to keep pace with her talents and the failed relationships. To amplify to her condition, she attached herself to more grief-stricken people. She identified with them and they identified with her. What they forgot was that the blind cannot lead the blind! This led to the beginning of "Phase I: The Great Depression of 2013."

She started to hate herself and completely underestimated her abilities. She looked around at everyone who was happy, failing to understand how they remained so. After months of sobbing into her pillow and thwarted attempts to get her relationship back, she realized she needed to talk and ask for help.

People who knew her as a roaring lion didn't understand her silence. But no one was able to reach to the depth and lend a hand, it was then when "Phase II: The Great Depression of 2013" took place.

She had read self help books, which did nothing for her. She had gone out for vacations and didn't feel normal or recreated. She tried to go to the gym and music classes, but all in vain. She just couldn't gather the confidence. She tried to study again, but stopped, as she didn't want to fail any more. She was living her fears and not her dreams. She didn't know what was stopping her:

her fear of failure, the lack of determination and hard work or the lack of passion for the choices she made.

When the endeavor to recover from Phase I failed, while living the disappointments in phase II, she entered deeper into Phase III. This was the phase of complete lack of self-belief. Usually, when people run to God, it is a phase when you think material lives are purposeless and you should escape the life and find God. She could feel God's presence with her. She could feel that He would give her a warm hug, so that she could sleep well like a child. She was still wondering if things would ever change. She wanted her material life back. She wanted to make peace with her inner self. She wanted to be the lion again. But she did not know how to do that.

She felt like she was completely ripped apart. She thought there was nothing to lose in accepting that she was lost when it came to her future and vision. She began talking to people and presenting her views without caring about what they would think of her. She was willing to tell people that she didn't want the corporate route. She liked watching plays more than cricket matches!

And then, a revelation dawned upon her. That was all she needed to do in the years to come – not care!

As they say, people spend their twenties and thirties thinking of what the world would think of their choices. By the time they are in forties, they realize that what they think is important, and also realize that the world never cared to think about them.

This is a realization. It can't be taught. One can only experience it when they want to, or when they actually do.

The freedom to express gave rise to: talking liberation, or the end of the Great Depression of 2013.

Chapter 7

Talking Liberation

Pihu's angel – i.e., her mother, and her freedom to express were her strengths now. She knew that she had the courage to make a start. Mothers never judge their children. She started talking again. She started getting out of the cocoon she had put herself into. She realized that people around you observe others – especially when they are weak. She didn't want to be judged. But now, she didn't care. She wanted to live again. She didn't want to behave like Henry Ford or Steve Jobs. She wanted to be herself, Pihu.

She now talked to everyone: old and new friends. As she talked, everyone listened. She had to work hard to challenge her comfort zone and her need for approval. But, she did it. People around her were exhilarating. They were facing new challenges, happily. Their courage surprised her. She couldn't understand the rock solid self-belief that they had. But they inspired her to try new things. She was in love with change then. She wanted to dream again. She wanted to dream big and walk into the unknown. She wanted to be just "she" for some time and not center her life on any one.

She had the power of optimism. She counted her blessings from her angel, for her friends and for her life.

That Memorable Touch

Miles and miles to walk,
So through many stages of life to many you talk.
Not all touches feel you deep,
Most through memory lanes sweep.
Then SHE fed in my mouth, now I eat with knife and fork,
Then SHE held my finger, now I walk with the folk,
SHE was the shinning angel in my life that did walk.
Time changes and life turns all over and again,
You look back to see, what you lose/gain.
Life is not easy, life's not plain,
You then remember the past,
You realize life moving so fast,
You remember the touch feeding you,
You remember the finger you held to,
You remember the words fed to your ear,
You remember HER hug of a bear.
The angel is still there when you need to talk,
But you carry on as there are.
As there are Miles and miles to walk.

Inspiration Spray

The man who pushed his stick from his mind,
The man who hated the stick for his daily grind,
He was a renegade of his kind,
He decided to stay as he wished.
He went to work passionately, no day he missed,
He read Drucker at 80, new ads he risked,
The man believed in today, not his future or past,
The man pushed his family to have a blast,
He had his speed and his race last.
He abhorred the nurse and hospital white,
He created his own medicines in his daily fight.
He didn't care about the body but any spirit blight,
My man, none other than, Grannie lay on bed.
Saw the victim attitude in me, and pounced instead,
He taught me to fight and had not fled.

Magic Dust

Best friends that they were,
In each others' lives happiness they stir,
Lot of talks from rise to set,
Being there in prosperity and debt.
They went on a rowing trip,
Exciting adventures they lost the grip,
Balance of connection kept them going,
Hope of togetherness didn't require any rowing,
Steadiness kept the boats from sinking,
Until one eye looked at the shore blinking.
He hurried to row and reach farther,
He believed courage her friend could gather,
She tried hard but was left behind,
Her friend was already at the shore line,
He was mad at her for not being fast,
He didn't know alone if she could last.
She shut her eyes to hear the hope,
Her belief in him was the pulling rope,
She listened to the voice with her eyes shut,
She rowed away in shower of his MAGIC DUST.

Pihu's support system - comprising her mother, her best friend and her grandfather, sprayed inspiration to her stinking stagnation. The scent added floral colors to her ambitions and beliefs. Finally, she made an executable action plan with achievable small goals to get out of the mired situation.

Goal one was to lose weight. She prepared a laundry list of exercises. She didn't enjoy such activities as gym and running. So, she started walking, but increased the amount of time that she spent in comparison to running. She researched on healthy and unhealthy foods, and decided that there was too much information to introduce everything all at once. She simply left out all the sugar and starches. In the first three months, she lost ten kilograms. This was her small, yet big success. Her bigger learning here was persistence without results. In the first month, she saw no result, but this time she decided to continue without letting anyone tell her what was right or wrong. She didn't share her plans with anyone and didn't subject herself to any judgment. It was important at that time, since she was not strong enough to take criticism. All this while, she also read about different things.

Goal two was to get in touch with her strengths and to rediscover the Pihu from high school and college. She wanted to meet the one who didn't fear living, whose gung-ho attitude would instill life even in coffins. This time, she created a reading plan which was sustainable. She pushed herself to read non-fiction books. She read autobiographies such as Open by Andre Agassi, My Experiments with Truth by Mahatma Gandhi, No Limits by Michael Phelps and others. She made notes on the techniques they used and applied them regularly in her own life. Some failed and some succeeded. She decided to get a dose of inspiration every day, either from people, videos or books.

Fight Back Charlie

Get up Charlie, don't feel lost,
Get up, it's time to heat the frost.
Jump and catch your distant goals,
Don't just watch it going away and scroll.
Get up Charlie, find a way out,
Step up even if you are in doubt.
Falling behind is not a defeat,
The marathon just wants you on your feet.
Don't faint away, listen to THE VOICE,
It's the final lap, it does hurt thrice.
Right track and success does offer cries,
Fight back Charlie, coz it's time to rise.

STEVE
STEVE

Beating Gravity

The Voice says, "Move from your comfort zone."
I didn't know how
I liked what I did.
Didn't understand what's wrong with it,
With every step I rise a bit.
Still…
It's my comfort zone and move from it,
I don't know how.
There is a gravity that pulls me in,
There is a charisma in every win.
There is a habit to beat defeat,
So, the VOICE, I shift + delete.
It's my comfort zone and move from it,
I don't know how.
As every saturation, bursts this bubble.
And THE VOICE multiplied in decibel,
The loudness became my escape velocity,
My core left the comfort zone and its gravity,
It's my comfort zone and I moved from it,
Listen to the sub-consciousness is how I did.

The Et (Extra Terrestrial) Way

I am in an ET zone,
Fluid at life, having no bone.
Meeting new people, sharing my plans,
Walking a path, with or without clans.
A funny guy I met on the ET way,
For him strategy is samosa in a tray
(Everyone has one).
Drink, Dance, laugh and he did live,
His fuel is smile and his act to Give.
Another one wants to live in Goa,
Is willing to quit banking to be a rower,
He wants to stop and live from scratch,
Fill answers in fast life's torn patch.
The third one wants to inspire a bn people,
Is throwing stones at still waters to ripple,
It's inspiring to hear his dreams and thoughts,
They are not just dreams but action well sought.
I am traveling, reading and listening around,
At last the rolling stone I found,
People don't see me, but my blue avatar,
Running and floating to the skies far,
I am in an in ET zone.
Fluid at life, having no bone.

Chapter 8

New Grounds

Pihu ventured into new avenues. She had her teen energies back. She packed her bag with confidence, exploratory spirits and dreams.

Her guarded adult fears were packed away. She began to live life king size. She decided to try everything she had once feared. She wanted to break free and see her horizons. She wanted to see her newness. She was more than ready for new challenges. This time, she was not afraid. She learned that experimenting kept all the moss of idleness away. Her agenda was to embrace all ambivalence. She finally became a fearless pilgrim in life. She danced to both, loud and silent music. She ran to milestones without prints. She tried to travel on the same road, but like never before.

Pihu stood up for herself many times. Would her exploration turn out to be a risk? She quit her job. She had limited money. She was traveling with strangers. Would this be the "change" that everyone spoke of? Would this experience be life-changing, for her?

A few months of her travel had passed. She went to Kashmir, Rajasthan, West Bengal and Hyderabad. She traveled in cars and trucks. Her mind wandered on her feet. Her steps were not counted. Her destination was not known.

But was all change good? Did she know all her elements and shades? Did she get dull with the sun, and grey with doubt? Did she get white with love? Did she know her addiction and her resistance?

Child In Me

Bumpy and jumpy, tumbling on my feet,
Loaded with joy, exploring new street.
Adult fears are away, the child in me is back,
Open embrace to people, dancing to their tune.
Rain is fun again, drenching like a toon,
Foolish courage is my steps, mountains or drums,
Laugh out loud, no fear of perception,
Making my own mistakes, firing away self doubt.
Ask stupid questions, child in me is back,
Disruption push is vital, childlike curiosity my spear.
Leaving the spell of over-thinking, action my swear,
Uncoiling the adult layers, child is me is back.

Back To School

Searching for more wisdom,
Intrigued by my questions,
Filling grey cavities.
Curious, I went back to school,
My bag had stones of baggage,
Heavy on my shoulders,
Dropped a stone with every mile.
Vicarious, I went back to school,
Association with ambitious people,
Introspection on my goals,
Reflecting on past and future.
Inspired, I went back to school,
Trying new ventures and plans,
Stemmed from need to create,
Endeavor to entrepreneur change.
Driven, I went back to school,
Away from bandwagon,
Un-herded I took disciplines new,
Learning to live, not for money.
Fearless, I went back to school.

Pihu had heard of Johari's Window from her peers. The window has four parts: an open or free area, a blind area, a hidden area, and an unknown or dark area. She knew that there are facets to one's personality that one only knows as well as others know; facets that only one knows; facets that only others know, and those that neither one nor others know. She wanted to know of all of her sides, whether blind or dark.

With the dream of wanting to see all her faults, and with her foolish courage in tow, Pihu made friends of all kinds in the new place. This time, she didn't put her filters into place. After all, she was living the dream – a life of change and new experiences! Her free-spirited attitude attracted everyone's attention. Before she knew it, she was in the company of free thinking people who, though, tended to take advantage of others. Her feet were shaking. She was dithering. So far, she had only been betrayed by love or by expected corporate politics, but not by friends. They made her see new lows in life. She was introduced to unsafe substances. She over-estimated her control over them. Was she guilty of exploring her dark side? Somehow, her mother's blessings and His hand sheltered her. In a matter of weeks, she discovered reality and found her senses. She made an immediate return to her known self. She saw her dark side. It was a face, not in the mirror, but hidden behind it.

Dark Side

Wings are spanned wide
Flight is long and unknown
Exploring my strengths
Astonished by weight, pulled
Pihu is living her bright side;
Testing unknown waters -
Easy to fly alone and with the likes,
Trying a different flock,
Different feathers, swans and ducks!
Pihu is ducking to pressure,
Her colors are changing to grey.
Did she know her dark side?
She knew her resistance but not lack,
knew her speed, but not inertia.
Pihu is no longer white.
Dark are the feathers,
The sky seems far.The lake seems deep
Float, fly or drown,
Identity lost or found,
Am I a duck or a swan?

Horizon

Ran for miles in dust and thorns
My feet don't understand petals.
They lost their stand, still finding balance
Running towards your lighting storm.
Every step is shackled with sins,
HE does not give horizon with ease.
Your light is too bright.
I just crawled from dark.
Trying slow and fast together.
Am stretching earnestly to reach,
Hoping to swing with the storm thrust,
Waiting with the wings spread,
Storm is over and pillar stood.
The wings were weak to lift.
To reach YOU I needn't be a pillar.
Sand I am, just carry me along.
Don't want land or water
Don't want a foundation strong
Don't want house or boat
Suspension in horizon is sound.

Chapter 9

Re-bottled

Years passed with Pihu and her diaries having their close conversations. She savored many different fruits that life offered her so far. She learned to find meaning in every experience. The anxieties of youth settled over the years, and shaped her into a more patient and tolerant adult. She went on soulful quests. She understood herself better. She was confident of what she wanted to do. She had her vision and her beliefs about life. She was not shaken by new ground, new territories, and new peopleanymore. She learned how to get up from nowhere. She learned to live without money, loveand direction. She imbibed ways to find new directions. Walking on those paths was not easy. It was difficult for her to make her family and friends understand what she wanted, always.

During her long travels, she read books and met people, encountered companies, and investors. She learned how courage, risks, and changes help one go forward. She started her journey towards one goal: change without fear. She wanted to kill all fear she had in her. She wanted to live a fearless life. She wanted to feel pressure and be able to respond with strength.

She decided to add planned disruptions to her life, once every two years.

Meanwhile, she met with another accident. When she was thirty-two, she met a rather quiet boy: Kabir. She wouldn't call it love, again. It was more than love. It was meaningfulness. His words didn't define her. They let her discover herself. They didn't live to look after each other. They lived to complete each other. They were very different in what and how they did things. But they respected each other and their individuality. They traveled together. They were at the stage of maturity where pretence was not required. Although they were both from Delhi, life was not about Armani and Gucci. They looked at experiences. There was a childlike connect in their relationship. They watched old movies and songs to relive their childhood. They shared enough memories from the past without envy or pessimism. They were differently colored, and angled, but fit each other well to complete the jigsaw.

Agile

Look for trouble
Cowardice won't help.
Rationalize approaches
Prejudice won't help.
Jump off cliffs
Mere heights won't help.
Learn from others' climb,
Envy won't help.
Falls add to agility
Mere rise won't help
Her falls give her spring,
She rises faster now.
Friction gives her persistence,
She aims higher now.
Strangers give her comfort,
She uncoils, deeper now.
Dark gives her familiarity,
She can find light her now.
Experiences enlighten her,
Her feet are resilient now.

Nine To Wine

I was nine and a grape,
Fresh with enthusiasm,
Sweet with ignorance,
High hanging and fenced firm.
My roots went deep,
To nourish me for the extra shine,
The stems kept me away,
Away from the stealers.
Seasons changed; so did air.
Mud losing its fertility,
Rains testing the brawn.
I curled and shrank,
Lost the golden twinkle,
Determined to stand still -
Scanning passing air and pollen
Couldn't find one to carry me,
Ageing, rotting, infected with pests,
Fermenting fast, no zeal no zest.
'Your' cast gives me the flavor,
Re-bottled from nine to wine.

Mirror You

From cracked lips to glossed smile,
From dark side to the childlike,
From predatory dreams to sound sleep,
From careless falls to watchful me,
Holding your hand, I reflect you.
From vulnerable days to independent me,
From ambiguous direction to concrete strokes,
From fidgety walks to confident waltz,
From a loud fighter to silent killer,
Learnt as your lady, I reflect you.
From unconscious mistakes to watchful actions,
From lack of trust to respect and love,
From doubtful dialogue to enigmatic story,
From lose clay to sculpted us,
I am your lady, I reflect you.

The Untitled Everything

You're the hand on my back,
When I burp.
You're the sand beneath,
When I drop.
You're the teacher around,
When I'm lost.
You're the naughty Jerry,
When I'm Tom.
You're the cozy blanket,
When I'm numb.
You're the caring mother,
When I'm a child.
You're the protecting father,
When I'm riled.
You're the pair of watchful eyes,
When I'm blind.
You're the stretching ladder,
When I'm short.
You're the soothing water,
When I'm in draught.
You're the listening son,
When I pretend to be wise.
You're everything to me,
When I'm just a wife.

Pihu established her own enterprise - a boutique value investing firm. She was able to multiply her savings by manifold and invested it well. She gave Kabir a lot of credit for convincing her to persevere. They inspired each other. She believed that God had His own pedagogy to train her to reach her goals. All cotton beds would have probably landed her in underutilizing her potential or perhaps, even being unaware of her potential. She happily takes risks and it keeps her adrenalin up. She regularly reflects on her journey, from Nine to Wine to keep her buoyancy alive.

Kabir is on with his own journey as well as the one with Pihu. They traveled twice a year to unwind and re-sow their magic. They were blessed with two sons. She didn't exactly call this a happy end to the movie. She had just tasted this unknown water and was preparing herself to row. Every day, for her, was like it was for a student. She was making notes to find a better approach. She lived with her extra pounds but didn't advocate them nor was she let down by them. She was capable of handling honest criticism and was matured enough to improve herself at her pace. She found an equilibrium with which she played by changing the forces in her life. At the end of the day, she did return to her equilibrium.